1983

THE RIGHT MOMENT

THE RIGHT MOMENT

MICHAEL PFLIEGLER

Translated by
Sister M. Veronica Riedl, O.S.F.

UNIVERSITY OF
NOTRE DAME PRESS

Library of Congress Catalog Number: 66-19031

Copyright © 1966 by
University of Notre Dame Press
Notre Dame, Indiana

Published 1960 as *Der rechte Augenblick,*
copyright © Verlag Herder & Co., Vienna.

Manufactured in the United States of America

Foreword

This essay came into existence as the result of a lecture before educators and instructors at all levels—from kindergarten to college. Since the audience was invited to discuss the material presented to them, that is, to formulate their objections, to contradict, clarify, and complement, it is possible to publish this book in a wider context than the original lecture.

I am well aware of the fact that nothing new is being offered to genuine practitioners in the field of education itself. It is merely that from long personal experience in dealing with youth and years devoted to research, I have gained a twofold insight that is both immediate and detached. Thus my approach is both human and scientific.

M. P.

Contents

I
THE RIGHT MOMENT

What Is Education?

We may begin by questioning what is meant in this study by the word "education." The German word *Bildung* (as differentiated from *Erziehung* or *Unterricht*) contains the word *Bild,* which literally means "image." The concept is similar to that of an image as it assumes form in the mind of an artist. A sculptor, for instance, visualizing a specific form, will set to work drawing it out of the stone; while contemplating his block of marble, he has all the freedom in the world to impose upon it whatever form he chooses. However, we recognize a fundamental difference here between the artistic formation of matter and the formation of human beings. This preconceived image toward which the creative process tends may not be as arbitrary in the formation of human beings as it is in artistic making. From the very beginning, organic matter carries within itself the seed of its final development. Living beings are, to quote Aristotle, *entelechien.* They come into being and develop toward their perfection in a given, absolutely

11

specified direction, which is not subject to any arbitrariness. An apple seed will necessarily develop into an apple tree, and no scientific genius can make it grow into a palm tree.

This directedness applies to man insofar as he is a living organism. Since man is a being endowed with spirit, his psychological and spiritual development is bound to his body-soul unity. He can have no image of himself other than as that of a *person*. Thus, the goal of education is the becoming of this person, this individual personality, raised within this specific culture.

Man is, above all, spirit gifted with understanding and freedom. It is precisely by means of these qualities that he distinguishes himself from other living organisms also directed toward a given end. Therefore, his fulfillment does not happen necessarily and without conscious effort. Education is his task. Because he is a free person, he can develop the true image of himself. However, this same freedom means he can, through his own fault, fail to develop as a man. Since he belongs to the tangible world of living organisms, he is, for the most part, master of the last and true fulfillment of his nature. For instance, he has the choice either to elevate and sublimate the dignity of his body or to deny this dignity. It belongs to him as man to be, body and soul, one being. Consequently, we do not say enough when we say that body and soul interrelate with each other. This relationship can hardly be explained as a mere side by side existence. Rather, soul and body interpenetrate, complement each other as the interior and exterior of the same entity, as being and expression *(anima forma corporis)*.

Spirit realizes matter.

Matter realizes spirit. They are partners acknowledging each other.

Education is the task of man endowed with freedom. True, he cannot choose his final goal, because it is already determined. He cannot want to be anything other than what he is. "Become who you are" may be paraphrased as "Become the You, whom you ought to be." The Greek ideal of personal development is expressed in the concept of *kalos k' agathos*—beauty and goodness—and the Roman's image of the whole man is *humanitas*. In the Gospel (Matt. 5:48) the natural powers of soul are seen in an astonishing new dimension of depth. In Genesis 1:26, the image of man "becoming man" is an image of God Himself.

In such a concept of the education of man all knowledge and capacities play the role of mere means. The danger of this kind of formalism can be avoided only if we keep in mind that only truth and pure insight into reality can educate, since there is a universal lawfulness the Creator has put into the totality of creation. Even a more imminent danger, in our day, is educational materialism. The general idea of education—even for the "educated"—is the passing of examinations, but we must not forget that one can pass all examinations without any real education of one's own nature. There are many graduated barbarians who have no sense of *Kalokogathia* or humanness—let alone Christian perfection.

The "Psychological Optimum"
in the Process of Education

Here we must introduce a new idea. All organisms develop according to a rhythm of growth—an organic, not a systematic development. The individual parts do not form independently, one after another, but in the context of the whole. Everything has its own time. Artificial interruption of this rhythm, as in a hothouse culture, is contrary to nature, resulting in infertility.

Although the formation of man, a personal being, does not depend entirely on a rhythm outside himself, it is at the same time not completely independent of such a rhythm. In any case, the law of becoming, growing and maturing, tiring and dying, governs human life as well. Now, the time most decisively influencing the final form of an organism is the time of its youth. It is then that the foundation, which is the outline of its possible perfection, is laid, although the organism may be influenced by favorable or unfavorable circumstances. Thus, by the end of his youth (in the middle twenties) a person is basically formed; from this point on he will not change radically. But throughout the process of his education, the teacher must be as aware of the law of timeliness as a gardener who knows the time for transplanting, for pruning or harvesting. Certainly, we cannot say that every learnable fact is bound exclusively to a specific stage of development, yet we must admit that every stage has its unique educational task. We call this favored moment in the accomplishment of a task the "psychological optimum."

It may happen that an educator, disregarding the rhythm of progressive maturing, makes premature demands upon his students. In other words, he expects more than the person is able to handle in this stage of his development. One need not be surprised to find the student either stunted, precocious or bored. Because the teacher presented an educational value at the wrong time, it merely skimmed the surface of the student's consciousness. But as an additional side effect, it left him insensitive to a deeper experience, as he now assumes the attitude of feeling equal if not superior to any given task without even sensing the weight of its importance. As a result he may become completely incapable of coping with the question, for its meaning, depth and power will remain a hidden reality for him. Thus, we may say that a law of psychological readiness and psychological resistance holds true in the field of religious education.

Disregard of this law may also result in retardation of the educational process. It may well happen that a man comes face to face with a truth or a task after its "due" date. A decision has already been made during a sterile and unhappy moment when the tremendous depth of the truth and the importance of the task were not at all realized. It may take great effort of will to reapproach the same point of decision later on in life. For instance, a man now realizes that, while he was at the crossroads, he chose the wrong path. Rarely does he decide to turn around and begin all over again. In the usual, concrete life situation he doesn't have the time to do this, because the present moment is the psychological optimum for the accomplishments of his immediate tasks.

How absolutely necessary it is for any educator to be aware of the developmental stages and specific periods of psychological readiness! However, should the student have passed the right moment without being opened to these possibilities, the teacher need not lose courage, for he knows what still remains possible and what does not. Above all, he must not act ignorantly, forcing students to produce results not fitted to their stage of development. If the teacher poses the problem too late, he may count on difficulties he would not have had previously. It may well be that certain possibilities are irrevocably passed, and only extraordinary will power or the grace of God can fill the lack.

Developmental psychological insights into human growth and into the significance of certain stages must be the presupposition of any educational endeavor.

II
THE THREE DECISIVE STAGES

The Three Decisive Stages

In my opinion there are three decisive stages in the formation or "education" of a human being. The first is that of childhood, when basic character traits are formed. During the second phase, adolescence, personality will either be established or be lost. In the third phase, young manhood or young womanhood, experiences of the world ripen into a definite *Weltanschauung*.

Speaking then in these general terms (and exceptions do exist), it may be said that childhood forms man as the "generic man," man among men, a creature within creation. Adolescence gives to this being a sharply defined personal individuality, depth and the power of responsibility. During his young manhood he assumes his place in the world, drawing together all of his insights and forming a unified view of reality that will govern all the further decisions of his life.

I am well aware that what I have said concerning the formation of man sounds fatalistic. However, the laws governing the very nature of the educational process cannot be invented, defended, or rejected. They are laws of the nature of man; as such, they must simply be known, encountered, and accepted. There is a law of life and a law of death. The fact that the law of dying shocks and frightens us does not change the reality of its existence.

However, we do not mean hereby to deny the freedom of the educator or the freedom of the subject to be educated. We merely wish to indicate points of reference that may help to avoid deceptions, as deceptions can easily lead to an attitude of carelessness. In the educational process the "right moment" is always a moment of freedom. Everyone knows of special hours of decision that have determined the future of a life or directed a destiny. Once the moment is passed, the decision has been made. Now there are certain phases in the educational process of every person's life that are no less decisive. A person may greatly desire to relive squandered or misused moments of his youth, but these moments will remain squandered and misused. Belated efforts may have moral value, but rarely do they lead to actual success, at least in regard to natural achievements. A person needs an extraordinary passion for reparation should he intend in later life to change his malformed character. Of course, grace can do all things, for with God "nothing is impossible" (Luke 1:36). Man, however, has only his possibilities and that is all.

Early Childhood

The Foundation of Human Ethics

In times past, educators paid little attention to the earliest stages of childhood. Evidently, crawling and playing seemed to be mere animal functions. The life of the spirit, if one could speak of spirit in the child at all, seemed limited to his recognition of the surrounding world and to play. It was said that a child understood nothing at this early age. Because his actions were instinctive and not consciously performed, a child could not be educated.

This opinion was commonly accepted until recent years. However, true mothers have always known that a child develops good or bad habits in the very first years of his life. With what concern a mother corrects any naughtiness, for she knows that bad habits would be very difficult if not impossible to eradicate later on. Nonchalantly we attribute great importance to this age when we say one person had a good upbringing and another person had a bad upbringing. We indicate that a person's upbringing affects his entire life, that indelible impressions are made in his childhood.

Since the dawn of depth psychology we have known that the first years of life are the most decisive in the formation of character. It is as though the frame of each person is then established; the face of his interior life along with the pattern of his relationship to others develops only within this frame.

Without a doubt, the education of the infant begins very early. Once I met a friend who looked very tired. I recalled that he recently had become a father, so I remarked: "Well, does the little one keep you up all night?" He answered: "Not at all. A child who spends his first nights in the hospital doesn't cry during the night because he finds out that crying is of little avail." This is actually true. At home, a mother will run to the crib every time the little one makes a noise. But the nurse in the hospital ignores the crying during the night; after some time the child stops crying, not because he draws a logical conclusion, but because, like an animal, he unconsciously perceives the answer of his environment. His response is likewise unconscious. Evidently, his behavior acclimatizes itself to possibilities available in his life. The same holds true for developing a pattern of moral behavior. It can be formed only in the experience of a "No," a limitation; or a "Yes," the fulfillment of a wish.

During the last decades a great amount of literature in the field of child psychology has been produced. Entire schools, for instance, have been dedicated to the findings of the toddler's stage. What we need today is an over-all view, enabling us to understand the early development of the child in terms of the total meaning of life. Amidst the many trees, we must again find the forest. Alas, many parents are as yet unaware of the very basic insights into child psychology and are, therefore, unable to apply them to the education of their children.

The first question that we, as educators interested in "formation," need to consider is the following: Since the framework of personality is established in the first years of life, what factors determine its character? It could be said that personality is grounded in the repeated experience of a limitation—the experience of order.

From the range of myriad experiential possibilities we might extract three typical instances. Capturing what is typical means attempting to channel the flow of life into some specific forms. Of course, beyond, below, and between these types there are other forms, because life is complex. But here are three typical cases:

1. The child *lacks* the experience of limitation, the "No."
2. The child experiences *only* the limitation, the "No."
3. The child experiences the *balance* of freedom and limitation, "Yes" and "No."

1. In the first case, every wish of the child is satisfied if not anticipated. As soon as the child manifests a desire, the mother runs to fulfill it. Worse yet, perhaps another person, hired to care for the child, has no other real task than to satisfy promptly every whim of the little one in his charge. Most probably, the hired person—the baby sitter—gives himself to the job with much dedication, but with little reflection. This very circumstance emphasizes a child's sense that he has an unlimited and uninhibited right to de-

mand. What does this mean in terms of the child? In his most impressionable, unconscious, and pliable time, the child lacks a profoundly basic life experience, namely, that desires have limitations. He never learns that there are possible and impossible things in life, things allowed and forbidden, legal and illegal, or that others, too, have desires and the right to assert them even against his own wishes. If, moreover, a child should find out that a baby sitter was scolded by the parents for not fulfilling his specific request, the consequences could be detrimental. The child sees that the person who contradicts his wishes does wrong. Apparently, scolding serves the baby sitter right. How does this idea affect the child further, we may ask. Such a child may well become demanding, insolent, saucy. Dominated by his own emotional drives, lacking self-control, he becomes naively passionate. On the other hand, he becomes passive in the face of his own desires since, until now, they have always been satisfied by someone else. He may become either inconsiderately brutal and cruel toward others or completely insensitive to their needs.

Later on, he interprets every limitation that teachers may impose upon him as an unjust impingement or as if they were stifling his life-energy. A few years ago we witnessed the following case in Vienna. A seventeen-year-old boy murdered his parents. They had loved him like an idol, fulfilling every one of his wishes. But then came a time of economic crisis and they could not give their son everything he demanded. Since he had known his parents only as caterers to his fancies, and since they now presented an obstacle to his acquisition of a half-million dollars' worth of life insurance, he simply removed the obstacle. As usual, the court ordered local investigations as to motivating causes. The deed was "officially" reconstructed as though the crime had no deeper roots than the occurrences of a preceding hour.

2. The second typical case presents the extreme opposite. The child's desires, even legitimate desires, remain unfulfilled. He experiences life in this most impressionable, sensitive, unconscious time only as a "No," a limitation. He conceives the world as hostility and opposition. "Order" means rigidity. It matters little to the

child if the harshness proceeds from the malice or from the plain stupidity of the persons involved. Just as he is unable to become morally guilty at this age, so is he unable to distinguish between intended cruelty toward him and the hard facts of a particular situation. Anyhow, bitterness sinks into his unconscious. What does this mean in terms of the development of the child? There may be various psychological reactions, depending on disposition, temperament, race, and hereditary traits.

One particular reaction manifests itself in a sadness of spirit. There are such broken people, incapable of experiencing any joy—they cannot even laugh. When they try to laugh, they feel as though they really shouldn't; they have no right to it, and their laugh turns out to be a grimace. Like beaten dogs, they sneak through life submissive, dependent, servile. When someone renders them a deed that any other would take for granted, they bend low and receive it like a grace. They simply expect nothing but rebuke and rejection from others. When life offers them a pleasurable moment, they simply lack the power to grasp this happiness. Such a slavelike attitude can be passed on from generation to generation as a family trait.

A second reaction to the exclusive "No" experience presents further danger. As the child grows up within a hardened and vulgar environment, he may feel that this hardness is directed toward him intentionally. With the premonition that he has a right to happiness, he sees in every man the antagonist who frustrates his possibilities to achieve it. He becomes hostile and distrustful, even to those who mean well. This grudge against the world enters his unconscious, and later on this man does not know why he hates the way he does. Unconsciously he seeks revenge; and when an opportunity presents itself, he does not discriminate in taking his revenge. He has no personal enemies: the existing order, humanity as such, all happy people are his enemies.

"Misery loves company" says an old proverb. How often men of the same disposition find themselves in groups only to fan one another's hatred. When we reflect that during various revolutions innocent and helpless people were cruelly murdered because of blind hatred, we wonder if the circumstance of the moment sufficiently explained this behavior. It seems, rather, that long-suppressed wells of hatred were suddenly set free to cause these inhuman atrocities. Every revolution or social upset seems to bring to the fore the unrestrained, the cruel type of man. Surprisingly, case studies reveal that these gruesome revolutionaries were usually shy and reserved men in their private lives, and no one belonging exclusively to their private lives suspected the kind of public behavior they had exhibited.

A third type of people whose justified desires have remained unfulfilled in early childhood resign themselves to their lot in the world. In reality, however, they are constantly fighting it within themselves. They have learned that to struggle against a given situation makes no sense and yields no success. The situation simply demands subjection, and besides, the world demands that the subjected one appear on the surface with a smiling face. But these people become unauthentic, deceitful, insidious, sometimes malicious. Although they have lost all faith and confidence in people, they give the impression that all is well. Although they hate their environment, they pretend to like it, lest the pressure become unbearable. These children become untrue in the very center of their being at a time when their interior life is in formation. Relationships with others partake of this inauthenticity. Since the child judges from his own untrue center, no man—not even the best—can be trusted.

Perhaps the most terrible consequence of the constant denial of pleasure is a seeking after hidden compensations. The child hitting upon some secret pleasure will throw himself headlong into it. The satisfaction this secret pleasure affords is heightened in the child's knowledge that other people may well forbid this pleasure but have no actual means to prevent him from enjoying it. The discovery that forbidden fruits always taste sweeter rests on such an unhealthy attitude. Thus, a child may become a habitual liar simply because he enjoys the confusion he succeeds in creating. This confusion is his revenge on the environment, and it gives him the satisfaction he craves. When he snatches and steals, it is not the stolen object that fascinates him, but the secrecy of this deceptive adventure.

Perhaps the child will become envious. But this envy is not a mere "suffering" because of the happiness of others; this envy displays a hideous and unnatural self-satisfaction. More frequently, however, a child of this disposition rejoices in the misfortune of another, until such rejoicing becomes his second nature. This kind of satisfaction seems to be the most readily attainable. Other children, themselves tortured and joyless, delight in finding ways to torture others, perhaps animals, perhaps the teacher. With unfathomable insight, they detect the point in which the teacher is either weak or helpless or bound by disciplinary laws. The teacher, then, becomes the innocent, impersonal victim of the child's need to release his frustrations.

3. It is hoped that the third typical case represents the majority. Here the child experiences the "Yes" and "No" as order. He recognizes that in this life "Yes" and "No," freedom and law, have a place. A mother who says "Yes" to the child at one time, and out of the same love says "No"

in a different situation, shows the child that the "No" is a necessary good in the world. In this way the child grows spontaneously into the awareness of order, the most essential presupposition of human existence. He experiences order before he even becomes conscious of its necessity. Order becomes a self-evident principle in his life.

How often teachers struggle with children who are interiorly confused and incapable of attention. Retracing their family history, we would probably find a broken home, a disagreeing father and mother who have ruthlessly pulled the child into their conflict. Torn in two, the child has not experienced the tranquility of order, and so he makes instability and confusion a way of life. There are also parents who try to rid themselves of their little "dependents" at all cost, and then wonder why their grown-up children insist on the same independence. In the rows of our classrooms today we face products of a dissolved and confused family life. Listlessness should not surprise us! The "only child" is especially in danger of becoming what we have characterized as the first typical case.

Why Should Malformation in
Early Childhood Be so Harmful?

It is a fact that the younger, the more impressionable, any organism, the more indelible will be the damage done to it. On the one hand, such a young organism can outgrow and, therefore, more easily overcome maladies. On the other hand, the soft condition of the plasma causes impressions to be stamped more deeply and to leave permanent scars. Although growth continues normally, something like a structural transfer has occurred, constantly influencing and co-determining the entire being. This process of natural growth is the same in man. "Every *first* remains forever in the child," says Jean Paul. We may say without doubt that all first impressions influence the entire life of man.

A second consideration follows. Based on common experience, borne out in a new way by depth psychology, it leads to basic principles of psychotherapy. Whatever a man assimilates unconsciously, be it good or bad, remains unconscious and cannot be brought to the surface. Therefore, sickness caused by the unconscious cannot be cured. Only in suffering the consequences of a sick unconscious can a person come to know the causes. A weakness of this kind cannot be cured even by making the matter conscious, simply because the disorder had never entered the psychic sphere in this way. The elements building the unconscious sphere of a man become like his second nature. Reflection doesn't help, for in self-study a man sees himself only as he is—with the weaknesses and abnormalities that have become part of his organism. Nor is he aware of them as being wrong, dangerous, or even strange. For what reason, then, should he fight them? Later perhaps, when further consequences call his attention to it, he will see the reason. And when he is finally forced to face the problem, it will seem that he is asked to do violence to his own nature. Just who is willing to undertake this?

A dilemma results from the fact that all educational method seems to be based on an obviously true statement: "The child does not yet understand!" True, but such a statement may be misinterpreted. A child, of course, does not understand if, by understanding, we mean the procession of autonomous moral insight and responsibility. Because the child does not understand, parents and educators need to know that a child assimilates their understanding. They must know that the child's moral foundation builds upon their ground, and that the image of what man ought to be should not be distorted. If this second nature, punctured in its foundation, begins to cause innumerable problems, an almost hopeless struggle begins—the struggle against the unconscious caricature of a man. It doesn't really matter what a man decides to do—take up arms against his own image or cast his disfiguration into stone—both alternatives will effect disturbances in human relationships. Yet, only in relating to others does a man discover his moral foundation. Understandably, then, the personally experienced "I" of adolescence is more easily drawn into awareness. Surprisingly enough, men can grow very old before they realize how asocial they really are. In summary, we may say, the sooner the impression is made, the more unconscious it is, and the more it affects the person.

In these early years a human being rests naively in the order or disorder of his immediate environment. Although order and disorder were, so to speak, outside the child at first, it was there they made a decisive impression upon him. This person, directed either toward order or disorder, then takes life into his own hands, creating order or disorder respectively. The fundamental orientation to order or confusion remains. Prospects of eliminating this rooted disorder are indeed minimal. Only in the period of adolescence—when the foundations of the human being are again shaken in their very depths—a basic rectification, or reorientation, seems possible.

The above reflections should focus our eye to the tremendous importance of a preschool formation. Society may neither ignore nor handle arbitrarily the problems of family life and preschool educational institutions. Kindergartens are a legitimate substitute for the family only when the organic family unity is lacking. Above all, it is the social womb of the family that exerts the most decisive influence upon the child. The family is, in the deepest sense, the cell of every community.

The first years of human existence are decisive for laying the foundation of basic human behavior; they are likewise decisive in establishing the child's basic relationship to the root of all being—God. This does not mean, of course, that the child is able to encounter God. It means, rather, that the framework for a possible encounter will take shape in these years.

A neglect of religious values within the first years of formation presents an almost irretrievable loss. Religious sterility or areligion has its source in this loss. From Jean Jacque Rousseau to Ellen Kay and Sigmund Freud, the need of the child's relatedness to God seemed of little concern. The religion of the child was thought to be a mere exterior, gesticular limitation of rituals. In fact, one feared to approach the child with religious realities at too early an age. This fear and reproach seem justified in view of the method through which the child was often approached religiously. Fundamentally, however, the thesis was erroneous, especially since experimental psychology has found that a child comes to the quest for God by himself. Sigmund Freud seems to be in error when he writes: "I think it would take a long time for a child not influenced by anyone to begin thinking about God and things beyond this world."

We should grant this statement the amount of truth it contains. However, we believe that one who, from a convinced atheism, finds nothing wrong in neglecting religious influence loses the right to the above statement. Anyhow, Jean Paul Richter seems to be the keener observer when he states in his "Levana": "Within the child dreamily slumbers the entire religious metaphysics. How would his interior visions of eternity, God, infinity, holiness, and so forth, be possible since these notions cannot be communicated through exterior means. To describe these notions we have only empty words which may evoke and awaken, but which cannot create." Similarly Edward Spranger states: "It may be assumed with certainty that religious life is not only put into the child, but that it also develops out of spontaneous drives." Spranger makes this statement rather cautiously, yet it does not mean he has any doubts at all as to his own insight. Although he believes that religion proceeds from the child spontaneously, he also believes that religious forms of expression are taken from the adult world.

However strange it may sound, child psychologists have found that a child between the ages of four and seven logically arrives at a notion of God as the last cause of reality. "By a logical process, the child arrives at the notion of the Initiative Who stands behind all things. Thus he is brought face to face with a basic notion of God."

Man's relationship to God is not arbitrary and cannot take arbitrary forms. By nature, religion is the soul and center of life. When relegated to the realm of luxury, religion is robbed of its essence and becomes essentially misunderstood.

When we consider the two truths just discussed—the fundamental importance of the first years of life and the fact that a child asks the question about God on his own initiative—we come to understand what deplorable effects an intended areligious or irreligious environment must exert upon a child. In a God-estranged atmosphere his most natural question is put aside; all religious impulses must necessarily suffocate in their core. Then the seed is planted for the religious blindness being experienced in large segments of our society.

During his first years a child becomes related to God in one of three ways: religion may become a matter taken for granted; it may remain an unanswered question—a question that will not be asked again until adolescence; finally, it may become a matter of no concern at all. In this last event a man sinks below the level of human existence. Since religion, an essential quality, has not been developed, psychological restructuring has occurred; and matters can be remedied only with great difficulty in later years. Certainly they are not remedied by a child's exemplary participation in religious exercises during the grade school years. These actions, performed without thought, will be dropped without a scruple as soon as the catechist ceases to demand them.

The first years of life not only decide

whether or not a God-I relationship will be possible, but also determine the "how" of this relationship. In other words, early childhood notions of God and experiences of God determine the God-I relationship definitively.

Anyone who has worked with adolescents knows they have notions of God that are rarely related to notions of life and energy. Rather, God floats somewhere above life. He is a Being far removed from real things, perhaps a Being that hovers over them. They encounter Him in a state of rebellion or fear. As a rule, this attitude toward God is determined by early childhood experiences. God does not make much of an impression on the child during his grade school years simply because in these years he has only a minimum capacity to experience Him. Perhaps, however, sometime in his early life God was used as a threat. This indeed is a most objectionable practice when considered from the Christian view of a Father-God. We need hardly ask about the effects of such an abuse. It could be that the child threatened this way already experienced the threat of the big black dog next door.

Because the child does not retain many impressions, the few that enter sink very deeply into his psyche. A transfer may occur, and "God" may take on all the fearful qualities of the big black dog. Although this image may slumber in his unconscious during the grade school years when emphasis is laid on religious functions, it will nevertheless break forth again during adolescence when the interior life returns once more in its spontaneity and freedom. Then this notion will become a problem. A distorted notion of God may turn religion into actual torture for some young persons. Others who have not experienced a certain cultivation of faith are now in danger of tearing the frightening image of God forever out of their souls because of misunderstanding Who He is.

An example may illustrate this point. Let us look at the importance of familial order in the formation of the God-Father concept. A first-grade teacher had laudably intended to proceed from natural experience in presenting the notion of God the Father. "Well," he said, "just what is a father like? A father cares for his family; he is good. When a child needs something or wants something, he may always go to his father." At this, one child in the class began to cry, saying: "My father is no good. He comes home drunk! When we go to him, he wants to hit us!"

How true that faith in God and in His providence is grounded in a family order! Parents and child may be completely unaware of what is happening. Yet, these home impressions are so deep that they are capable of directing the religious attitudes of later life. The importance, then, of forming the right notion of God can hardly be overemphasized. It should not be left to chance; nor should it be left to the hands of untrained babysitters who need to use forceful threats to maintain peace and quiet. It is likewise important to know when and where the concept of God is formed. The research of E. Noberling gives clues: "A child experiences God in dreams, in prayer; he experiences God in need—sickness and death, thunderstorm, the sense of fear and personal sinfulness." Noberling's research, though not directed toward the small child, may nevertheless be applicable here. It is of the utmost importance to interpret thoughtfully these events in which the God-experience may occur.

Usually a child formulates the explicit question about God between the ages of four and seven. While he is incapable of "reflecting," he can nevertheless visualize concepts in depth. Because his concepts are few, every single concept makes a deep impression. One could say that a notion accompanies, or pursues the child. William Stern, one of the best child psychologists, recounts the following case: "Someone had told a five-year-old the story of creation. Though the child asked no specific questions, a problem had obviously stirred in his mind. While in the bathtub one evening some days later, he made the unexpected comment: 'Funny, how God could make Himself. If God made everything, who made Him then?' He received the answer that nobody had made God, that God always is. The thought had occupied the boy for days. A child can play, paint, work at something for hours and then—at a most prosaic time, like the time to wash—he will arrive at a solution." Stern adds this comment: "A five-year-old, independently, has discovered the idea of

50

Adolescence

Personality

Adolescence decides the personality of a man. This, of course, does not mean that at the end of adolescence a finished human being or personality has been produced. Rather, adolescence determines whether a person will ever become a personality or not. In the juridical sense every man in possession of his faculties who knows what he wants, or thinks he knows what he wants, may be considered a person. A philosophical definition of person, for instance the one Boethius has given us, says merely in very general terms that a person is a single, spiritual, individual being—*rationalis naturae individua substantia*. But personality seems to be more than that. Personality is person actualized, a person developed in his uniqueness, in all his depth, width, and wholeness. Each man is given the perfection of his unique nature as a task, and it is very important whether or not he achieves it. "All happiness of the children of men depends on fulfillment" (Goethe). If the person remains split and stunted, his lifework will be the same. *"Agere sequitur esse,"* a norm from the Aristotelian-Thomistic philosophy of life, remains valid. Only true personalities master life and the task which life has entrusted to them.

A man who has not grown into a personality will never experience his own natural perfection, and his work will rarely go beyond the banal unconscious level of routine. Should a people as a whole fail to educate personalities, this people may easily fall prey to progaganda slogans or any other power. The destiny of a country is not so much determined by the many, the all too many, but by the few who are whole persons.

Personality as understood in this context is neither a moral nor a religious concept; it refers to an achieved freedom and maturity. Religion and morality gain acceptability when made the concern of personalities rather than as statistics and statistician.

Adolescence as Phenomenon

We are not at the moment questioning the extent that puberty is a physical process and how far it is psychological. Adolescence designates an all-encompassing human process during the ages of thirteen or fourteen to fifteen. Between maturing of the body and maturing of the soul there exists, of course, a certain harmony but not a complete interdependence. This interrelation during adolescence is actually no different than at any other period of life, but since life-powers as such are forcibly amplified during adolescence, the forces exerted by interrelation are likewise more emphatic.

The most general statement that can be made about adolescence is this: Adolescence is a time of transition from childhood to adulthood. This transition period is the most important stage of a man's life. It is interesting that primitive man honors this time in extended cultic initiation ceremonies. In a civilized society, on the other hand, a youth fumbles rather blindly into adulthood—even during an age that has produced outstanding works in developmental psychology and pedagogy, as well as in every phase of adolescent behavior.

Perhaps the most uncomfortable characteristic for teacher and student alike is the instability of the adolescent. Nothing seems permanent. He is simply unreliable and without character. Progress occurs in leaps and spurts; regressions occur and are again superseded. Very naturally the youth gives expression to his rapid interior changes. Today he appears insolent, challenging, and daring. Tomorrow he is helpless and closed. Once he is more than self-confident—he is heroic. Another time he suffers inferiority complexes and acts like a coward. Again he will exalt his intellect and scorn all feelings, but the day before he was swayed and governed by his feelings for hours. And the next day it will probably be the same. Behind all these external manifestations an essential depth development is taking place.

1. The discovery of the ego. The unconscious existence of childhood as well as the group existence of grade school are

realities of the past. The ego begins to loosen itself from its ties to the immediately surrounding world. The youth experiences his own uniqueness. Facing his own existence, he realizes that he alone holds responsibility for himself. Along with this sense of responsibility for self, the capacity to think and to judge independently is also awakened. This proper right of the ego is experienced as a most unique value. But in the enthusiasm of the discovery this value may be overrated. Also, the newly found self-awareness may not be recognized in its "newness" by the surrounding world. In fact, it may be overlooked and ignored. But these boys and girls, hungering for attention and acceptance, defend themselves against being ignored. Boys become irritated and angry; girls are constantly "being hurt." They may become resistant and contrary should attention and acceptance be denied them. An educator intent on breaking this resistance by means of force only awakens greater opposition, interior defiance, and at times actual revolt. The adolescent knows that children are treated with methods of force, and he certainly does not want to regress into childhood. He does not want to be treated like a child. His opposition to authority should be seen in this context. It is first of all conditioned by the stage of his development—biologically conditioned—therefore, it should not be judged and punished purely by moral standards.

2. The discovery of the interior life. Just as childhood may be characterized by the discovery of the exterior world, adolescence may be characterized as a discovery of the interior world, which enables the person to come to himself and to be in himself. The riddles of existence come to the fore with a powerful concreteness. Yet nothing evokes the adolescent's self-awareness as much as his power to ask essential questions. Thus, he will ask them cloaked in a daring language. When he senses that his questions concerning the secrets of life embarrass the adult, or make the adult in any way insecure, his bold and daring attitude only receives encouragement. At times the young person finds in this embarrassment and insecurity a forceful means to tyrannize the teacher. Rarely if ever does a young person reach the conclusion

that a teacher's inability to answer his questions points to his own limitations or the senselessness of the posed question. He experiences his question existentially, not intellectually, for he does not yet realize the limitations of the human spirit; on the contrary, he magnifies his capacity to an unreal proportion. Although self-assertion grows at first into an irresponsible over-estimation of self, it is nevertheless necessary, because the young person simply cannot yet assume the full responsibility for his existence. If he does assume his responsibility before time, the result will not be a man with the proper self-awareness, but a revolutionary who acts out of a malformed psychological structure.

A symptom of the discovery of the inner world is the ability to daydream for hours. The young person delights in imagining what his future life will be. He is very generous and magnanimous in his dreams, for he does not yet know that the chances to realize dreams are sizably reduced in the face of reality. Rather, it is precisely in facing the hard facts of life that contempt or exaggeration takes form in his imagination. In imagination he rehearses his professional role, his achievements, his successes. How easily he overcomes the opposition of the envious and the difficulties enemies put into his way! In all these imaginative dialogues he emerges as the victor. Yet this preoccupation with a future profession drains many young people to the extent that they become incapable of paying full attention to their present tasks. A boy then becomes a lone wolf, and the "grown ups" don't understand him anymore. He doesn't understand them either. In fact, he even despises them. What do they know about his world when they live in their comfortably confined square. Curiously enough, many adults seem to forget their own youth completely and are incapable of understanding the interior difficulties that young people experience.

During the time of adolescence nearly all young people become creative in one way or another. Some paint, some write poetry, some develop fantastic plans in their minds. Art exhibits of high school students often evidence great power of expression. A few years later, however, these talented artists become ordinary clerks working in department stores on Main Street. The diaries of girls display an enthusiasm, a sensitivity and delight they will never again be able to express with the same passion.

3. The revolutionary trend. The radicality of youth is explained more by dissatisfaction or lack of moderation (though that is part of it too) than by a metaphysical hunger to reach the bottom of things. All the existential questions pressing to the surface at this time take hold with the power of the eternal. Thus, a creative and sensitive person may well develop on the level of spiritual depth. He may be unable to comprehend that people can take the obvious and everyday things so seriously, for he sees only the faraway horizon; he loves the unattainable. Reading Plato, he doesn't understand at all why he should bother with formulas and syntax. *"Eros uranios"* has taken hold of him. The professor then sees a person who desires to re-create the world but who considers the discipline required as unnecessary and invalid.

He sees another person who with the same vitality develops intuitive powers that will never be his again, who asks extraordinary questions and receives answers that never satisfy. There are three general reasons for this:

a. He is asking profound questions concerning human existence, and the answers to such existential questions can hardly be reduced to a reasonable formula. He has difficulty in accepting this, especially since his mind-capacity has grown and has filled him with an unbounded self-consciousness.

b. No answer can correspond to the passion and the intensity with which the question is asked.

c. A young person rejects finished solutions. He loves the state of change; he wills to doubt. (Here lies the essential difference between the adolescent and the young adult. The young adult strives to achieve peace and security.) Girls especially may pose great problems to a religion teacher, asking one question after another, but not really caring to hear the answer to any of them. How should the teacher expose the senselessness of the question; how should he answer?

This metaphysical hunger, though not

satisfied with a temporary solution, may throw a young person into an unbearable abyss of helplessness. His only salvation seems to lie in self-assertion, however un-justified. Otherwise he very likely may fall victim to a metaphysical disgust, which in some serious cases has led to suicide. He may also develop a fixed hostility toward all half-solutions, all limitations—however reasonable—against all half-measures, compromises. To adults this seems extremely foolish. But is it?

A comfortable contentment with the immediate and useful appears likewise detestable and disgusting to youth. One youth movement coined the slogan that later gained political significance—bourgeois. It should not be overlooked today that this attitude of the past century's youth was directed not merely against the satisfied material bourgeois, but especially toward the more dangerous spiritual Philistine who rested securely in his enlightened view of the world. Youth has attacked the positivism of E. Mach and its philosophy of life, as well as rationalism and its proud system.

Young people love danger; they desire

to experience the adventures of life, the danger that life holds on the level of depth. For this reason Freidrich Nietzsche easily becomes their hero as well as their danger. Danger results because daring proceeds more often from a lack of heroism than from true courage. Even more important, danger results because their radicalism is undirected in its source. A boy does not first become fired by a great ideal and then proceed toward its realization. It is rather the other way around. His whole attitude is radical, but he is yet undecided as to how he should use this energy. Therefore, he is easily drawn by the first thing that lures him. It is important, then, to harness his daring courage and abounding energy to the right wagon.

d. To interest young people in ideals is not a very difficult task. Their radicalism is nothing else but a loud witness to the human dynamism directed toward the eternal. Youth has not yet forgotten how to express this with courage. Ready and open for ideals, youth finds a philosophical idealism pale and too modest at times. Though they may make wrong choices of heroes and ideals, they are searching and open. If educators do not understand how to present a vital ideal to them, they will find their own. They will search among life-values because life, which now has taken hold of them, communicates a relatedness to all living beings, to all values of life: peoples, blood, honor, heroism, deeds, sport. Nothing seems further removed than the past, past events, traditions. How can they value something that needs numerous proofs for the right to exist, something that is not proven simply by the power of its presence. How can they value something that needs to defend itself constantly? For the young person a living ideal seems more convincing than a proven one. Is this not the case with adults also?

The Meaning
and Goal of Adolescence

As we have said, man's personality is always in the state of becoming. The years of adolescence decide the possibilities of development. A personality is marked by self-awareness, self-government, freedom, and uniqueness—all this in the most possible fullness, depth, and broadness. Only a man who has achieved maturity can be a support to a maturing youth.

Personality is the "I" distinguished from the We and the You. Personality means awareness of the "I" capacity to assume responsibility for the "I." A personality need not be a man with a great deal of knowledge. It is rather the man who can form an opinion, make a judgment; the man who understands his own position, is sure of his insight but open to any new aspect. Such a man has an overview of reality. He penetrates the words of the Lord: "What does it profit a man if he wins the whole world but loses his life. What can a man give in exchange for his life?" (Matt. 16:26). He understands the meaning of these words in their human dimension even if he is an unbeliever. All the turmoil accompanying the first discovery of the ego, the irritation provoked in protecting this newly born "I," the hunger for understanding, bids for attention and acceptance, the contrariness and stubbornness mean only this: the young person needs to protect the ego, to secure the "I" —the receiver of an independent existence and responsibility for the becoming personality.

If the "I" could not find its own depth, it would remain suspended in an empty gesture. Self can be true to itself only by earning this fidelity. By running from one party to another, from one amusement to another, some people show that they lack an interior life. Maybe, during adolescence, they missed the call to discover the inward man. Perhaps they have put aside their youthful dreams. Their ambitions to achieve something in life may have been exchanged for the romanticism of a Karl May. Some young people have been lured out of their depth into the diffusive open spaces where they live not their own youth,

71

but the youth of another. A man cannot live *an* ideal; he must live *his* ideal. Not having found their own ideals, some people have never grown beyond their youth; they have not come of age. In the intellectual life, they do not exceed the level of the grade school child. The grade schooler knows his lessons; later on he reads his newspaper, repeating only what he reads without ever forming an opinion. While this is perfectly acceptable behavior for a child, it is unworthy of an adult. A person so stunted senses the ridiculousness of his situation and, therefore, reads the paper out loud and with a conviction that only betrays his inability to stand within himself.

So many people remain children because they understood the time of "coming to self" as an illness rather than a task to be solved at that moment. Forever they remain apprentices of life; age and graying hair only make their situation the more tragic. In a decisive moment they have failed to experience life as a risk, and now they have only one fear, that is, the fear to risk. And they have only one wish: to be able to eat and drink in peace and security. Society makes ample provision for the necessary diversion and entertainment. It is possible for a white-haired man to die without even having noticed that he has not yet begun to live *his* life.

Viewed theologically, the radicalism of youth is nothing but the necessary drive toward the final questions of existence and the final security of life. A personality who does not find the meaning of his existence in his eternal destiny may be likened to a meteor racing through space in contrast to a cosmic body having its place in the cosmic plan of God. Admittedly, we hold in awe some so-called great personalities in history: conquerors who spurned the law, brutal self-worshipers who despised other men. But their greatness is that of a Tamerlane or a Genghis Khan, their personality turns into a curse for themselves and others.

At one time in his life, during his youth, man is confronted with the God from whom he proceeds. And though he may be a coward at all other times in life, during the years of his youth he *knows* the courage to face the ultimate risk of life, and he knows, too, that therein lies his final fulfillment and blessing. How tremendous must be the cowardice of the person who has not dared face this risk even in his youth. And how unauthentic he remains if, instead of having faced the risk with honesty, he has merely learned to mimic the "tough guys."

Yet, the assertion that youth is basically irreligious or antireligious has foundation neither in scientific research nor in everyday experience. True enough, religious forms of childhood must be shed; childish concepts of God must make way for a mature understanding. However, religion is not lost during the time of adolescence. Rather, adolescence is the time during which a truly personal relationship to God is made possible. Two reasons for this may be given:

1. The young person is thrown into a state of confusion, a condition of weakness never experienced before. No one, no other person, can be of actual assistance to him. Out of his own need he finds God as the Savior, experiencing Him for the first time as *his* God and Lord. The second reason seems even more applicable to youth:

2. In his radical attitude, the youth ex-

74

periences the dynamic thrust of human existence toward God. Provisional answers do not satisfy him, and his search is a real one. A teacher in a vocational school where the teaching of religion was prohibited allowed his students from time to time to ask questions concerning their life problems. Of course, religious questions were prohibited in order to avoid denominational controversies. But the students, filled to the brim with religious questions, urged him until he agreed to discuss this subject. It seems that adolescence presents us with a "psychological optimum" for the religious formation of man. Thus, the trend to reduce or omit religious instruction altogether during this time should be opposed. Rather, religious instruction ought to be introduced where it is lacking today. Youth needs to know; youth searches for the meaning of existence. Should the most important question be left to a chance answer, or a casual comment? Rather, would it not be better to guide youth toward an all-encompassing answer? Naturally young people need attentive listeners with much patience and love.

Only a wise educator who understands adolescent instability can counsel with all seriousness, and only such is qualified to give religious instruction. A detailed and complete teaching of dogma or moral principles seems irrelevant at this time. In particular educators should avoid all theological speculations unrelated to the decision of faith. What matters most is that the young person know himself confronted with the most central truths of his faith, that he experience the depth and power of these truths in his whole humanity, that he grasp the significance faith has in building his life. A youth has little longing for philosophical theories of faith; he longs to be addressed with the existential truths affecting his life. When his radicalism does not find a master in the depth-sphere of his faith, when faith is presented as something narrow or as merely an unreasonable demand, he is then in danger of losing his faith. Instead of teaching Christian morality as violence done to oneself, teachers ought to present it as the fulfillment of one's best self. Moral education must always refer to the freedom of conscience.

On the other hand, it should be emphasized at all costs that religious instruction needs to present a wholeness of the Church's teaching, for the greatness and completeness, the summation of truths and realities, must shine forth. The achievement of this triumphant and integral picture puts an extraordinary weight of responsibility on the catechist. Single truths or the image of the whole may both be forgotten by the student. But when an eighteen-year-old realizes his faith in such manner that he knows he can risk life only in faith, something has been reached— something has happened. A detailed knowledge is not important now because the Christian personality has come into being. To acquire more knowledge and to refine the concepts are tasks of young adulthood.

It is obviously erroneous to suppose that every adolescent will lose his faith or at least doubt it. In many cases faith continues to live, frequently because of effective religious instruction or because of dissatisfaction with poor instruction.

At the end of adolescence a person does not stand securely in a final order; but by reason of his basic decision, he may stand directed toward an order, toward the one God. He may also stand titanically directed against the order. At this crucial time he decides if his life is to be lived in unworthy debasement or with individual responsibility, if life is to be lived in stagnation or with human dignity—that dignity which every people and individual receives from God as a gift and a task. These crucial years decide, too, if a person will lead an impersonal herd-existence or if he will treasure the dignity of man as personality.

The risk and the uncertainty of adolescence are motivating factors for some educators to save the young person from the attending tumult of the years. This can be done only by sacrificing the full human dignity. Either a half-made, eternally unfinished man emerges, or the tumult rises again in later years. When the latter happens, the person is in grave danger; he is like an adult stricken by a child's disease. The attempt to guard the young person from making decisions is in most cases self-deception on the part of the educator. Occasional fits of anger may be avoided, but the young person loses thereby the means to free himself from self, and the educator loses every possibility to help him. Everything "seems" to be in order, but with the termination of adolescence, the "quiet boy" is worse off than his neighbor because he is more helpless.

One thing remains to be achieved: to give decisive clarity and order to his life. This is the task of young adulthood— another decisive time of life.

Young Adulthood

The development of responsibility as the expression of inner fullness, order, and perfection is one goal of education. But education implies more than that. A truly educated person is able to take an over-view of reality and, in a sense, to dominate it as far as possible; this he accomplishes from an integrated, personal center. We hold that a person who has gained such an open perspective on reality has a *Weltanschauung*. A child recognizes his surrounding world merely as a collection of things arranged next to one another or behind one another, but he is not yet aware of relationships. At most, a unity is conceived during the grouping together of various conceptions. As the person matures, this sense of an intrinsic unity between the inner and the outer world also grows. In fact, finding this unity becomes his special task. It may occupy him so extensively that he loses his sense for the immediate, common things at hand. With only a hazy premonition of a *Welt-anschauung*, all his powers tend toward this very fundamental decision. In this fog his search for direction, for an acceptable image of the world, may be compared to the atmosphere of a cloudy, stormy night. At one moment the world is all darkness; then again the world seems suddenly bright. The young person feels he is being pursued through a wide forest of ideas and data; while being knocked about, he gathers an impression of the eternal reality —but he never has a sense of peace and security, a sense of having found a permanent place in this universe. Nevertheless, to secure an intellectual existence becomes not only a possibility but also a duty for the young adult.

This stage of young adulthood (from ages 19–24) distinguishes itself from adolescence (14–18) in many respects. While the adolescent has fought his environment by having protected his own ego, the young adult—sure of his selfhood—is searching for his place in the world. Wanting to be a revolutionary, questioning everything— all this gives way to the seeking of an answer, a final answer. The adolescent had craved to be lonely; in a sense, had to be lonely. But the young adult, grounded in self-awareness, is seeking a partner, a "You." While the adolescent had purposely shunned people in authority, the young adult is realizing that without them and their help he cannot even begin his life's work. He does not care to doubt on principle; he now prefers to seek security.

The dilemma of the young adult lies in this. At the time when he would be able and willing to form his own *Weltanschauung*, he leaves high school, losing perhaps the only systematic way of acquiring one. At this time he also decides his profession: he chooses his school, his subjects, his field of specialization. Thus, he runs the danger of limiting himself to a mere segment of reality when he most needs to form a liberal over-all view of reality as the basis for his consequent life-decisions. He can, of course, overcome the danger. In fact, this limitation imposed by specialization may intensify the need and desire for a unified *Weltanschauung*. Besides, the situation necessarily prevents him from thrusting his view of reality into the clouds; that, of course, could happen if his sphere were all too narrow. Yet, more frequently, the young adult must take his education into his own hands. It may happen that a certain accidental experience or the very narrowness of his chosen sphere imposes itself upon the meaning of all reality. A science, an art, the enthusiasm for a certain ideal takes the place of a religion. Conscientious research concerning one unique aspect of some notion can fulfill such a "scientific life" completely. Then we have the type of man whom Ortega y Gasset calls "the knowledgeable ignoramus."

Various countries attempt to counteract the danger in various ways. In German universities *Weltanschauung* courses have been introduced. The "Studium generale" above and beyond specialized training remains a topic of discussion. In nationalistic Spain, General Franco has made the daring suggestion to establish introductory courses to the Catholic religion on the university level.

This is not a medieval and queer gesture of regression. It can be supported by developmental psychology, which postulates a "psychological optimum" for the building up of a *Weltanschauung* during the years of young adulthood. It must be understood, however, that all attempts of this kind will lead to success only with the consideration of the degree of independence and freedom due to this stage of human growth.

Only after graduation from high school do problems concerning this essential, intellectual life-decision arise. Although signs of these problems are noticeable during the junior or senior year, the year most psychologists label as critical seems to be the age of eighteen. Stanley Hall and E. Starbuck observed that public school youth breathing a secularized air (the air of business competition), without ever attending formal religious instruction, experienced within their seventeenth year of life either a "conversion to faith" or a final conversion to the materialism of the Western world. After research, Hildegard Hetzer fixes the critical age between sixteen and nineteen, the nineteenth year being one of temporary solution. Charlotte Buhler sees the most intense period of religious struggles around the age of sixteen and seventeen, leading to the crisis during the eighteenth year.

What do we mean by crisis in this context? The term as it is used in the field of medicine signifies the climax of an illness, a turning point to a condition either better or worse. The religious decision, at the climax of a certain psychological development, presents a turning point from adolescence to adulthood. At this point a man may become truly religious or fail to give his life religious significance, fail to achieve the openness to dedicate himself radically to a great ideal. However, the metaphysical hunger of adolescence will not easily return. His life may become shallow before it has begun.

At the age of nineteen, a period of stagnation may set in. The cause for this may be threefold: either the young person has already overcome his problems, or he has vainly exhausted himself in the struggle or—and this is the most common—the turmoil of adolescence recedes, questions remain unanswered, and all that results is an all-pervading superficiality.

Anyone can observe in everyday life these results of scientific psychological research. The student who graduates from high school with a definite well-rounded *Weltanschauung* is the exception. During the high school years a student should be exposed to the purpose and seriousness, the depth and the width of a Christian view of reality. The young person should have found confidence and a central focal point from where he can grasp what is essential, distinguishing it from what is not essential. Should religious instruction fail to be convincing with regard to this point, then all single premises become meaningless because the center of faith is put into the state of doubt; it expresses a newly created orientation of the mind.

In Catholic students the decision for faith stretches over a longer period of time, according to many noted religious psychologists. Therefore, colleges must assume the greater responsibility for forming a *Weltanschauung*. The final education of a man depends on the college or comparable institution. Time will show if and how colleges will succeed in the integration of this total view of reality with the transmission of professional and vocational skills. Education is only complete when a comprehensive philosophy of life has been found.

The young adult has just become capable of integrating his ideas and notions. The given, the objective, reality has just taken on meaning for him. Only now does

90

he have his powers under the control that is needed in order to unlock multiple routes of inquiry. With his whole being he tends to make his existence secure. He likes idealism as a philosophical and ethical norm. It seems relevant to mention here young Socialists who repeatedly introduced themselves to a discussion group with the words, "But we are not Marxists!" What they meant to say was that they did not adhere to a materialistic *Weltanschauung*. Otto Turnlirz makes the observation that the *Weltanschauung* decision may be of two varieties. It is either an aesthetical idealism or a religious idealism. In other words, man becomes either religious or chooses an idealistic philosophical background for his life. It may also happen that a value such as the destiny of his people becomes his dominating motivation. At times of great national tumult, all questions—including religious ones— are judged, solved, or rejected by evaluating them in relation to the destiny of the patriotic community. This kind of situation intensifies the impact of the religious decision. No flight into generalities, such a flight as intellectuals like to take, will be possible then.

A condition of stagnation, a lack of questioning, may lead to religious immaturity. Here, religious questions remain unsolved, on a childlike level. This infantile religious view of reality does not correspond to the intellectual development of the person on other levels; it must, therefore, be rejected. The cause of this rejection is not religion, but the ridiculous level of religious education.

The Educational Crisis on
The College Level

The present educational crisis on the college level may well be provoked by a neglect to form the *Weltanschauung* of students. Some colleges, like factories, produce bachelor's, master's, and doctor's degrees in a very mechanized fashion. The goal of the student is to achieve a specialized skill in order to get a job as quickly as possible. This pragmatic attitude seems to be miles removed from the thinking of great teachers—for instance, Aristotle, when he says: "Parents should educate their children, not because education is especially useful or indispensable, but because it is proper to man and a noble, good thing to do. It does not seem dignified for the free man to ask constantly if what he does is useful" (State VIII). The educational task of the college can be nothing other than calling the student to freedom. He must hear the call to freedom and experience the inevitability of the call. Someone must point out to him the dangers of

a specialized training and show him ways and means of reaching a unified view of reality and truth above and through specialized studies.

Some colleges have in the past promoted such integrated programs. Traditionally nondemocratic states of Europe began to demand an education for the whole man, not only for his intellect. They guarded themselves against a liberal idealism that shuns responsibility; they fought for compulsory education and responsible academic freedom. They fought against a presumption that scorns every desire for existential security; they tried to eliminate the estrangement between the academic and the people's world.

In these strivings the will to renewal becomes evident, although a new danger of one-sidedness must be recognized. The goal of all scientific endeavor must be intensification of insight and the extension of its truth, as Max Planck has repeatedly stated. Honesty and propriety of thought, conscientiousness and respect for the modes of knowing proper to each discipline— these must always be maintained.

Educating the whole person can be done

only from a point where the freedom of man is respected as well as his essential bond with eternal values. A right decision regarding the matter can proceed only from a truly religious attitude. The educated person emerges from the process of all our intellectual, moral, religious thoughts and acts—and from an achieved order of life. Thus, the way to this perfection has three critical moments in the development of the young person, and recognition of these moments decides whether or not the goal of fulfillment will be reached.